A DON'T SWEAT THE SMALL STUFF *Treasury*

A Special Selection for Graduates

Richard Carlson, Ph.D.

A Don't Sweat the Small Stuff Treasury
A Special Selection for Graduates

FIRST EDITION

10 9 8 7 6 5 4 3 2 1

Contents

⸺⸎⸻

Introduction

So often when I think back to the proudest moments of my life, they were the times when I had graduated from something I had worked hard at completing—high school, college, graduate school, or a course or program signaling the end of a process. To this day, I love attending graduation ceremonies when someone I care about is being honored with a diploma. I love seeing the pride and excitement in the eyes of the graduate, to witness their sense of accomplishment and to share in their joy.

Frequently, during ceremonies, graduation is described not so much as an ending but as a new beginning, a chance to branch out, expand one's horizons and explore new opportunities. With the skills and knowledge that have been achieved, a graduate is encouraged to "take on the world" with enthusiasm and courage.

Along with the joys and benefits of graduation, however, come new challenges and hurdles to overcome—a new set of worries, responsibilities, concerns, plans, and things to think about. It's no wonder that graduates often feel stressed out, despite their recent accomplishment! Therefore, I think it's particularly important for graduates to learn to stop sweating the small stuff. With all the excitement and new possibilities surrounding graduation, it's in a graduate's best interest to keep the little things from taking over his or her life. This will allow them to keep their eye on more important issues, as well as to enjoy, rather than stress out over, what is yet to come.

It's for this reason that I have created this little book especially for graduates. I've carefully selected strategies from each of my *Don't Sweat the Small Stuff* books that I feel are most appropriate and, hopefully, most useful for the challenges that seem to come with new beginnings.

If you are a recent graduate, I send you my sincere congratulations and very best wishes! I hope you are filled with pride, both today and for years to come. Undoubtedly, you've worked hard and you deserve your success. I hope that, along with your success, you'll also be able to keep things in perspective and experience the joy of a happy and contented life. I hope this book is helpful to you in creating peace within yourself.

Treasure the gift of life,

Richard Carlson

teach you to be less judgmental.

Your job is to try to determine what the people in your life are trying to teach you. You'll find that if you do this, you'll be far less annoyed, bothered, and frustrated by the actions and imperfections of other people. You can actually get yourself in the habit of approaching life in this manner and, if you do, you'll be glad you did. Often, once you discover what someone is trying to teach you, it's easy to let go of your frustration. For example, suppose you're in the post office and the postal clerk appears to be intentionally moving slowly. Rather than feeling frustrated, ask yourself the question, "What is he trying to teach me?" Maybe you need to learn about compassion—how hard it would be to have a job that you don't like. Or perhaps you could learn a little more about being patient. Standing in line is an excellent opportunity to break your habit of feeling impatient.

You may be surprised at how fun and easy this is. All you're really doing is changing your perception from "Why are they doing this?" to "What are they trying to teach me?" Take a look around today at all the enlightened people.

Surrender to the Fact that Life Isn't Fair

A friend of mine, in response to a conversation we were having about the injustices of life, asked me the question, "Who said life was going to be fair, or that it was even meant to be fair?" Her question was a good one. It reminded me of something I was taught as a youngster: Life isn't fair. It's a bummer, but it's absolutely true. Ironically, recognizing this sobering fact can be a very liberating insight.

One of the mistakes many of us make is that we feel sorry for ourselves, or for others, thinking that life *should* be fair, or that someday it will be. It's not and it won't. When we make this mistake we tend to spend a lot of time wallowing and/or complaining

3.

Allow Yourself to Be Bored

For many of us, our lives are so filled with stimuli, not to mention responsibilities, that it's almost impossible for us to sit still and do nothing, much less relax—even for a few minutes. A friend of mine said to me, "People are no longer human beings. We should be called human doings."

I was first exposed to the idea that occasional boredom can actually be good for me while studying with a therapist in La Conner, Washington, a tiny little town with very little "to do." After finishing our first day together, I asked my instructor, "What is there to do around here at night?" He responded by saying, "What I'd like you to do is allow yourself to be bored. Do nothing. This is part of your training." At first I thought he was kidding! "Why on earth would I choose to be bored?" I asked. He went on to explain that if you allow yourself to be bored, even for an hour—or less—and don't fight it, the feelings of boredom will be replaced with feelings of peace. And after a little practice, you'll learn to relax.

Much to my surprise, he was absolutely right. At first, I could barely stand it. I was so used to doing something every second that I really struggled to relax. But after a while I got used to it, and have long since learned to enjoy it. I'm not talking about hours of idle time or laziness, but simply learning the art of relaxing, of just "being," rather than "doing," for a few minutes each day. There isn't a specific technique other than to consciously do nothing. Just sit still, perhaps look out the window

8

and notice your thoughts and feelings. At first you may get a little anxious, but each day it will get a little easier. The payback is tremendous.

Much of our anxiety and inner struggle stems from our busy, overactive minds always needing something to entertain them, something to focus on, and always wondering "What's next?" While we're eating dinner we wonder what's for dessert. While eating dessert, we ponder what we should do afterward. After that evening, it's "What should we do this weekend?" After we've been out, we walk into the house and immediately turn on the television, pick up the phone, open a book, or start cleaning. It's almost as though we're frightened at the thought of not having something to do, even for a minute.

The beauty of doing nothing is that it teaches you to clear your mind and relax. It allows your mind the freedom to "not know," for a brief period about what's wrong with life. We commiserate with others, discussing the injustices of life. "It's not fair," we complain, not realizing that, perhaps, it was never intended to be.

One of the *nice* things about surrendering to the fact that life isn't fair is that it keeps us from feeling sorry for ourselves by encouraging us to do the very best we can with what we have. We know it's not "life's job" to make everything perfect, it's our own challenge. Surrendering to this fact also keeps us from feeling sorry for others because we are reminded that everyone is dealt a different hand, and everyone has unique strengths and challenges. This insight has helped me to deal with the problems of raising two children, the difficult decisions I've had to make about who to help and who I can't help, as well as with my own personal struggles during those times that I have felt victimized or unfairly treated. It almost always wakes me up to reality and puts me back on track.

The fact that life isn't fair doesn't mean we shouldn't do everything in our power to improve our own lives or the world as a whole. To the contrary, it suggests that we should. When we don't recognize or admit that life isn't fair, we tend to feel pity for others and for ourselves. Pity, of course, is a self-defeating emotion that does nothing for anyone, except to make everyone feel worse than they already do. When we *do* recognize that life isn't fair, however, we feel *compassion* for others and for ourselves. And compassion is a heartfelt emotion that delivers loving-kindness to everyone it touches. The next time you find yourself thinking about the injustices of the world, try reminding yourself of this very basic fact. You may be surprised that it can nudge you out of self-pity and into helpful action.

4.

Life Is a Test. It Is Only a Test

One of my favorite posters says, "Life is a test. It is only a test. Had this been a real life you would have been instructed where to go and what to do." Whenever I think of this humorous bit of wisdom, it reminds me to not take my life so seriously.

When you look at life and its many challenges as a test, or series of tests, you begin to see each issue you face as an opportunity to grow, a chance to roll with the punches. Whether you're being bombarded with problems, responsibilities, even insurmountable hurdles, when looked at as a test, you always have a chance to succeed, in the sense of rising above that which is challenging you. If, on the other hand, you see each new issue you face as a serious battle that must be won in order to survive, you're probably in for a very rocky journey. The only time you're likely to be happy is when everything is working out just right. And we all know how often that happens.

As an experiment, see if you can apply this idea to something you are forced to deal with. Perhaps you have a difficult teenager or a demanding boss. See if you can redefine the issue you face from being a "problem" to being a test. Rather than struggling with your issue, see if there is something you can learn from it. Ask yourself, "Why is this issue in my life? What would it mean and what would be involved to rise above it? Could I possibly look at this issue any differently? Can I see it as a test of some kind?"

If you give this strategy a try you may be surprised at your changed responses. For example, I used to struggle a great deal over the issue of my perception of not having enough time. I would rush around trying to get everything done. I blamed my schedule, my family, my circumstances, and anything else I could think of for my plight. Then it dawned on me. If I wanted to be happy, my goal didn't necessarily have to be to organize my life perfectly so that I had more time, but rather to see whether I could get to the point where I felt it was okay that I couldn't get everything done that I felt I must. In other words, my real challenge was to see my struggle as a test. Seeing this issue as a test ultimately helped me to cope with one of my biggest personal frustrations. I still struggle now and then about my perceived lack of time, but less than I used to. It has become far more acceptable to me to accept things as they are.

5.

Search for the Grain of Truth in Other Opinions

If you enjoy learning as well as making other people happy, you'll love this idea.

Almost everyone feels that their own opinions are good ones, otherwise they wouldn't be sharing them with you. One of the destructive things that many of us do, however, is compare someone else's opinion to our own. And, when it doesn't fall in line with our belief, we either dismiss it or find fault with it. We feel smug, the other person feels diminished, and we learn nothing.

Almost every opinion has some merit, especially if we are looking for merit, rather than looking for errors. The next time someone offers you an opinion, rather than judge or criticize it, see if you can find a grain of truth in what the person is saying.

If you think about it, when you judge someone else or their opinion, it really doesn't say *anything* about the other person, but it says quite a bit about your need to be judgmental.

I still catch myself criticizing other points of view, but far less than I used to. All that changed was my intention to find the grain of truth in other positions. If you practice this simple strategy, some wonderful things will begin to happen: You'll begin to understand those you interact with, others will be drawn to your accepting and loving energy, your learning curve will be enhanced, and, perhaps most important, you'll feel much better about yourself.

6.

Turn Your Melodrama into a Mellow-Drama

In a certain respect, this strategy is just another way of saying, "Don't sweat the small stuff." Many people live as if life were a melodrama— "an extravagantly theatrical play in which action and plot predominate." Sound familiar? In dramatic fashion, we blow things out of proportion, and make a big deal out of little things. We forget that life isn't as bad as we're making it out to be. We also forget that when we're blowing things out of proportion, *we* are the ones doing the blowing.

I've found that simply reminding myself that life doesn't have to be a soap opera is a powerful method of calming down. When I get too worked up or start taking myself too seriously (which happens more than I like to admit), I say to myself something like, "Here I go again. My soap opera is starting." Almost always, this takes the edge off my seriousness and helps me laugh at myself. Often, this simple reminder enables me to change the channel to a more peaceful station. My melodrama is transformed into a "mellow-drama."

If you've ever watched a soap opera, you've seen how the characters will take little things so seriously as to ruin their lives over them—someone says something to offend them, looks at them wrong, or flirts with their spouse. Their response is usually, "Oh my gosh. How could this happen to me?" Then they exacerbate the problem by talking to others about "how awful it is." They turn life into an emergency—a melodrama.

The next time you feel stressed out, experiment

7

Think of What You Have Instead of What You Want

In over a dozen years as a stress consultant, one of the most pervasive and destructive mental tendencies I've seen is that of focusing on what we *want* instead of what we *have*. It doesn't seem to make any difference how much we have; we just keep expanding our list of desires, which guarantees we will remain dissatisfied. The mind-set that says "I'll be happy when this desire is fulfilled" is the same mind-set that will repeat itself once that desire is met.

A friend of ours closed escrow on his new home on a Sunday. The very next time we saw him he was talking about his next house that was going to be even bigger! He isn't alone. Most of us do the very same thing. We want this or that. If we don't get what we want we keep thinking about all that we don't have—and we remain dissatisfied. If we do get what we want, we simply re-create the same thinking in our new circumstances. So, despite getting what we want, we still remain unhappy. Happiness can't be found when we are yearning for new desires.

Luckily, there is a way to be happy. It involves changing the emphasis of our thinking from what we want to what we have. Rather than wishing your spouse were different, try thinking about her wonderful qualities. Instead of complaining about your salary, be grateful that you have a job. Rather than wishing you were able to take a vacation to Hawaii, think of how much fun you have had close to home. The list of possibilities is endless! Each time you notice yourself falling into the "I wish life were different" trap, back off and start over. Take a breath and remember all that you have to be grateful for. When you focus not on what you want, but on what you have, you end up getting more of what you want anyway. If you focus on the good qualities of your spouse, she'll be more loving. If you are grateful for your job rather than complaining about it, you'll do a better job, be more productive, and probably end up getting a raise anyway. If you focus on ways to enjoy yourself around home rather than waiting to enjoy yourself in Hawaii, you'll end up having more fun. If you ever do get to Hawaii, you'll be in the habit of enjoying yourself. And, if by some chance you don't, you'll have a great life anyway.

Make a note to yourself to start thinking more

8.

Acknowledge the Totality of Your Being

Zorba the Greek was said to have described himself as "the whole catastrophe." The truth is, we're all the whole catastrophe, only we wish that we weren't. We deny the parts of ourselves that we deem unacceptable rather than accepting the fact that we're all less than perfect.

One of the reasons it's important to accept all aspects of yourself is that it allows you to be easier on yourself, more compassionate. When you act or feel insecure, rather than pretending to be "together," you can open to the truth and say to yourself, "I'm feeling frightened and that's okay." If you're feeling a little jealous, greedy, or angry, rather than deny or bury your feelings, you can open to them, which helps you move through them quickly and grow beyond them. When you no longer think of your negative feelings as a big deal, or as something to fear, you will no longer be as frightened by them. When you open to the totality of your being you no longer have to pretend that your life is perfect, or even hope that it will be. Instead you can accept yourself as you are, right now.

When you acknowledge the less than perfect parts of yourself, something magical begins to happen. Along with the negative, you'll also begin to notice the positive, the wonderful aspects of yourself that you may not have given yourself credit for, or perhaps even been aware of. You'll notice that while you may, at times, act with self-interest in mind, at other times you're incredibly selfless. Sometimes you may act insecure or frightened, but most often you are courageous. While you can certainly get uptight, you can also be quite relaxed.

Opening to the totality of your being is like saying to yourself, "I may not be perfect, but I'm okay just the way I am." When negative characteristics arise you can begin to recognize them as part of a bigger picture. Rather than judging and evaluating yourself simply because you're human, see if you can treat yourself with loving-kindness and great acceptance. You may indeed be "the whole catastrophe," but you can relax about it. So are the rest of us.

9.

Become an Early Riser

I have seen this simple, practical strategy help many people discover a more peaceful, even a more meaningful life.

So many people wake up, rush to get ready, grab a cup of coffee, and charge out the door to work. After working all day, they return home, tired. The same is usually true for men and women who stay home with their children: They get up just in time to start doing things for the kids. There is virtually no time for anything else. Whether you work, raise a family, or both, for the most part you are too tired to enjoy any time left for you. As a solution to the tiredness, the assumption is often made, "I'd better get as much sleep as I can." So, your free time is spent sleeping. For many people this creates a deep longing in the heart. Surely there must be more to life than work. children, and sleep!

Another way of looking at your fatigue is to consider that a lack of fulfillment and a sense of being overwhelmed both contribute to your tiredness. And, contrary to popular logic, a little less sleep and a little more time for you might be just what you need to combat your sense of fatigue.

An hour or two that is reserved just for you—*before* your day begins—is an incredible way to improve your life. I usually get up between 3 and 4 in the morning. After a quiet cup of coffee, I usually spend some time doing yoga and a few minutes of meditation. After that, I will usually go upstairs and write for a while, but I also have time to read a chapter or two in whatever book I'm enjoying.

Sometimes I'll just sit for a few minutes and do nothing. Virtually every day, I stop whatever I'm doing to enjoy the sunrise as it comes up over the mountain. The phone never rings, no one is asking me to do anything for them, and there is nothing I absolutely have to do. It's by far the most quiet time of the day.

By the time my wife and children wake up, I feel as though I've had a full day of enjoyment. No matter how busy I am that day or whatever demands there are on my time, I know I've had "my time." I never feel ripped off (as so many people unfortunately do), as if my life isn't my own. I believe this makes me more available for my wife and children, as well as my clients at work and other people who depend on me.

Many people have told me that this one shift in their routine was the single most important change they have ever made in their lives. For the first time ever, they are able to participate in those quiet activities they never found the time to do. All of a sudden, the books are getting read, the meditation gets done, the sunrise is appreciated. The fulfillment you experience more than makes up for any sleep you miss out on. If you must turn, off the television at night and get to sleep an hour or two earlier.

10.

If Someone Throws You the Ball, You Don't Have to Catch It

My best friend, Benjamin Shield, taught me this valuable lesson. Often our inner struggles come from our tendency to jump on board someone else's problem; someone throws you a concern and you assume you must catch it, and respond. For example, suppose you're really busy when a friend calls in a frantic tone and says, "My mother is driving me crazy. What should I do?" Rather than saying, "I'm really sorry but I don't know what to suggest," you automatically catch the ball and try to solve the problem. Then later, you feel stressed or resentful that you are behind schedule and that everyone seems to be making demands on you. It's easy to lose sight of your willing participation in the dramas of your own life.

Remembering that you don't have to catch the ball is a very effective way to reduce the stress in your life. When your friend calls, you *can* drop the ball, meaning you don't have to participate simply because he or she is attempting to lure you in. If you don't take the bait, the person will probably call someone else to see if they will become involved.

This doesn't mean you never catch the ball, only that it's your choice to do so. Neither does this mean that you don't care about your friend, or that you're crass or unhelpful. Developing a more tranquil outlook on life requires that we know our own limits and that we take responsibility for our part in the process. Most of us get balls thrown at us many times each day—at work, from our children, friends, neighbors, salespeople, even strangers. If I caught all the balls thrown in my direction, I would certainly go crazy—and I suspect that you would too! They key is to know when we're catching another ball so that we won't feel victimized, resentful, or overwhelmed.

Even something terribly simple like answering your phone when you're really too busy to talk is a form of catching the ball. By answering the phone, you are willingly taking part in an interaction that you may not have the time, energy, or mind-set for at the present time. By simply not answering the phone, you are taking responsibility for your own peace of mind. The same idea applies to being insulted or criticized. When someone throws an idea or comment in your direction, you can catch it and feel hurt, or you can drop it and go on with your day.

The idea of "not catching the ball" simply because it's thrown to you is a powerful tool to explore. I hope you'll experiment with this one. You may find that you catch the ball a lot more than you think you do.

Give Up on the Idea that "More Is Better"

We live in the most affluent culture the world has ever seen. Estimates are that although we have only 6 percent of the world's population in America, we use almost half of the natural resources. It seems to me that if more were actually better, we would live in the happiest, most satisfied culture of all time. But we don't. Not even close. In fact, we live in one of the most dissatisfied cultures on record.

It's not that having a lot of things is bad, wrong, or harmful in and of itself, only that the desire to have more and more and more is insatiable. As long as you think more is better, you'll never be satisfied.

As soon as we get something, or achieve something, most of us simply go on to the next thing—immediately. This squelches our appreciation for life and for our many blessings. I know a man, for example, who bought a beautiful home in a nice area. He was happy until the day after he moved in. Then the thrill was gone. Immediately, he wished he'd bought a bigger, nicer home. His "more is better" thinking wouldn't allow him to enjoy his new home, even for a day. Sadly, he is not unique. To varying degrees, we're all like that. It's gotten to the point that when the Dalai Lama won the Nobel Prize for Peace in 1989, one of the first questions he received from a reporter was "What's next?" It seems that whatever we do—buy a home or a car, eat a meal, find a partner, purchase some clothes, even win a prestigious honor—it's never enough.

The trick in overcoming this insidious tendency

is to convince yourself that more isn't better and that the problem doesn't lie in what you don't have, but in the longing for more. Learning to be satisfied doesn't mean you can't, don't, or shouldn't ever want more than you have, only that your happiness isn't contingent on it. You can learn to be happy with what you have by becoming more present-moment oriented, but not focusing so much on what you want. As thoughts of what would make your life better enter your mind, gently remind yourself that, even if you got what you think you want, you wouldn't be one bit more satisfied, because the same mind-set that wants more now would want more then.

Develop a new appreciation for the blessings you already enjoy. See your life freshly, as if for the first time. As you develop this new awareness, you'll find that as new possessions or accomplishments enter your life, your level of appreciation will be heightened.

An excellent measure of happiness is the differential between what you have and what you want. You can spend you lifetime wanting more, always chasing happiness—or you can simply decide to consciously want less. This latter strategy is infinitely easier and more fulfilling.

Ask Yourself "Why Should I Be Exempt from the Rest of the Human Race?"

A number of years ago I was complaining to a friend of mine about how much responsibility I had and how difficult my life seemed to be. His response played a role in my transformation from seeing myself as a victim of circumstance to being a person who truly accepts life as it is (most of the time). Rather than commiserating with me and sharing his own difficulties, his question to me was, "Is there some reason why you think you should be exempt from the rest of the human race?"

He was referring, of course, to the obvious, but largely overlooked, fact that life is full of challenges, obstacles, hurdles, setbacks, difficulties, hassles, and problems—for all of us. No one is exempt. Regardless of your background, race, religion, or sex—regardless of what kind of parents you had, your birth order, how much money or notoriety you have, and all the other specifics of your life—you will have problems. Case closed.

It's always easier to see your own problems than those of others, and it's certainly true that some problems appear to be far more severe than others, but the truth is, ultimately no one's life is particularly easy, at least not all of the time. The old saying is still true, as it will be forever: Circumstances don't make a person, they reveal him or her.

It's very helpful to remind yourself of this fact of life. It puts things in perspective. When we remind ourselves that life wasn't meant to be hassle-free or perfect, we are more able to respond to our challenges with perspective and grace. Rather than being annoyed or overwhelmed by every little thing, we're usually able to say something like "Oh, well, here's another one to deal with."

I doubt very much that any of us will get to the point where we enjoy the inherent hassles of life, but I'm certain that we can learn to be far more accepting. And, as you can imagine, the less you struggle with your problems and challenges, the more energy you have at your disposal to solve them. Rather than exacerbating the issues you are dealing with, you'll see the bigger picture, including the best possible solutions at hand.

Reminding yourself of the inevitability of problems to deal with won't make your life perfect, but it will put things in a healthier perspective and make life seem a whole lot less overwhelming. Starting right now, see if you can view your current problems in a new light. You might discover that at least the "small stuff" can be experienced with a great deal more serenity.

Go Camping

On the surface, this may sound like an odd suggestion, but I'm absolutely serious! If ever you wanted a strategy that would virtually guarantee to help you regain appreciation for your home and its many conveniences, this is it. And, to top it off, you'll have fun too.

I have a friend who once spent a summer taking underprivileged children on backpacking and camping trips. The trips were designed to, among other things, heighten their appreciation for their everyday lives. He informed me that the trips were a smashing success. As the kids were exposed to the beauty (and hard work and inconvenience) of nature, they returned with a new sense of gratitude for the homes they had been blessed with—regardless of how simple their homes might have been. I've found that the identical result is achieved when I take my family on a camping trip that might be as short as a few nights. Invariably, we return home with a more humble and gracious attitude.

When you're out in the wilderness, the simplest things—the things we normally take for granted—are far more involved; cooking, heating water for coffee, getting comfortable and settled for sleep, cleaning up, taking a shower, and reading at night, to name just a few. In fact, something as simple as going to the bathroom can become quite a chore. Depending on where you are camping, you have to either hike to the bathroom or, in some cases, dig your own hole.

Don't get me wrong. Camping is loads of fun

obnoxious to the manager of our apartment building. He felt he was right and that his attitude was more than justified. He believed that our requests were not being adequately addressed, and in a threatening tone, he demanded greater service. Whether he was correct in his assessment or not was irrelevant to the end result. Regardless of who was to blame, he had made an enemy. The problem was, we lived in a college town where there were virtually no empty units. Essentially, we were stuck.

From that moment on, our slow service became almost nonexistent. If the furnace needed fixing, we were last on the list. When the refrigerator was leaking, it took weeks to get it repaired. If someone parked in our designated spot, it was our problem to solve—and the manager wouldn't get involved.

What my roommate didn't understand was that, in all likelihood, our manager had been doing the ing as possible. As difficult as it can be to remember, landlords and managers have lives of their own, including many personal problems. I'm not defending landlords, nor am I at the time of this writing a landlord myself. I'm simply suggesting that it's *always* in your best interest to have a landlord on your side. If he or she is, more often that not, he or she will do anything within reason to make your life at home as comfortable as possible.

Dealing with landlords is one area where it's absolutely in your best interest to "not sweat the small stuff." The more perspective, kindness, and patience you exhibit, the more your landlord or manager is going to be inclined to be of service to you. The next time you have an issue to deal with that requires your landlord's involvement, try a little experiment. Let him or her know that you're aware of how busy he or she must be and how much you appreciate his or her help and hard work. Be kind, gentle, and patient. Do this not out of an attempt to be manipulative but simply because you are a kind, understanding person. Then sit back and observe what happens. You might be surprised at how much better your service becomes. Good luck.

15.

Think of Something You Did Right Today

Just for a moment, think of how often you calculate, keep track of, or think about how many things you do wrong in any given day. Things like "I can't believe I misplaced my keys, showed up later for my son's class, forgot to pick up sandwich stuff, missed the first ten minutes of the soccer game, forgot to make that important phone call, messed up, dropped the ball, failed to deliver, made her angry," and on and on.

Now, shift gears and think about how often you give yourself credit for doing something right. If you're like the vast majority of people I know, your ratio of criticisms to compliments is going to be weighted heavily toward the negative.

to sweat the small stuff. It puts your attention on all that is wrong with yourself and the world and makes you feel less than okay, even incompetent. Negative focus generates negative energy and, I believe, feeds into negative behavior. It reminds you of problems, hassles, and inconveniences. It makes you feel uptight and encourages you to be critical and hypersensitive.

When you think of things you do right, however, it brings your focus back toward the good in yourself. It reminds you of your competence and good intentions. It encourages you to give yourself a break and to make allowances for the few little things you do wrong or need improvement on. When you remind yourself of the things you do right, it helps you become a more patient person, with yourself and with others. It helps you recognize the effort and overall positive batting average that most of us experience, the fact that, despite our mistakes, we do most things pretty well. Rather than seeing yourself as a mistake maker, you'll see yourself (and everyone else too) as a character who is doing the best you know how.

Perhaps more than all of this, however, is the fact that focusing on what you do right makes life a lot more fun. It makes you less serious and rigid, and helps you feel less pressured, as if someone is keeping score of your efforts. My suggestion is this: Do the best you can in all aspects of your life, and then let go of it. Regardless of how hard you try, you're still going to make your share of mistakes. Once you accept this fact of life and put more attention on your strengths than on your weaknesses, you'll start having more fun that you ever dreamed possible.

16.

Become Clutter-Free

As simple as this suggestion is, it's worth discussing. And as simple as it sounds, it's actually not an easy task. It's taken a great of persistence, but I'd estimate that I have eliminated more than 90 percent of the clutter in my life. I'm convinced that this effort has helped me immeasurably in becoming a more easygoing person, as well as in my desire to stop sweating the small stuff at home!

Virtually every day, different forms of "stuff," much of which is useless and only takes up physical and mental space, comes into our lives. Without a concerted and conscious effort to counter this accumulation, we end up with piles and piles of useless junk to contend with. The reason: Clutter comes into our life whether we want it to or not. So, if we don't have a method of getting rid of at least as much (on average) as is coming in, it's inevitable that the piles will become ever larger and more difficult to sort through. Many people fool themselves that they will "get to it soon" or fall prey to the (almost always) false belief that they may need it someday. This latter excuse is validated by remembering a time or two when they needed something and found it buried under stacks of boxes in the back of the garage.

Clutter includes anything and everything that takes up space, distracts our attention, is irritating and in the way, or is practically never used. Some of the most common forms of clutter are piles of junk mail, scraps of paper, old newspapers, phone books, magazines, clothes and towels we no longer use, gifts and other items we don't know what to do with, old bikes and exercise equipment, piles of unused scrap lumber, nondeductible receipts, keys we no longer need, toys the kids never ever play with, old letters and other mail, books that we have either read or don't intend to read, memorabilia and other so-called sentimental things, knickknacks we don't even like to look at, excessive dishes or pots and pans, silverware and other kitchen goods, and so forth. When you get right down to it, most homes are filled to the brim with stuff that does little else than fill up space. I've been in many homes where the closets were absolutely filled up with things that were never used and where there wasn't even an intention of using a single item in the closets. And when I've been brave enough to ask the question "Why do you keep all this stuff?" the answer was usually something like "Oh, I don't know, we've always had it."

I believe that the reason so many people end up letting clutter take over their lives is that they never felt or experienced the joy of a clutter-free home. Most people, in fact, had parents who did precisely the same thing. Often, the first time an attic is cleaned is when a person dies or is forced out of a home for health reasons.

There is, however, something incredibly peaceful about a clutter-free home: opening a closet and actually having space to hang up something; opening a drawer without having to use force; being able to find virtually everything you look for; having open, airy space where there is nothing at all. There is something effortless and pleasant about sitting at your desk and being able to see the surface and to find your address book. There is something equally freeing about opening a kitchen cabinet and being able to choose easily and quickly from your favorite pots and baking trays without having to sort through and push back as if you were trampling through a thick forest.

Becoming clutter-free is an easy way to simplify your life and to feel more organized and in control. It gives you a peaceful feeling of space. It lifts your emotional spirit by giving you a feeling of openness and of being connected to, rather than over-whelmed by, life.

You can begin in simple ways—empty out drawers and closets. Give things away to people who will actually use them. Have a garage sale, and rather than keep the things you don't get rid of, give everything that's left to your favorite charity. Cancel any magazines you don't actually read and recycle all the ones you have kept. Go through your senti-mental things and create *one* special box for the things you'd really like to save—and give everything else away. Go through your clothes. Do you really wear them all? If no, wouldn't it be nice to give the things you don't wear to someone who will? And couldn't you use the tax deduction anyway? Maybe you could implement a new clothing rule: If you haven't worn it in two years, give it away today!

Most people who try to simplify their lives in this way are thrilled at the result. For some, it becomes a way of life that seems easier to manage. For others, it's simply an exercise in making their lives a little easier. I've found that as I accumulate less and get rid of the things I don't actually use, I truly appreciate those things that I do decide to keep. I hope you'll give this strategy a try, because if you do, my guess is that you'll be glad you did.

17

Never Miss a Chance to Say "I Love You"

In my lifetime I've heard many people complain that their parents (or their spouses) either never or seldom said (or say) "I love you." On the other end of the spectrum, I've never heard a single person complain that his or her parents, or anyone else, said these words too often.

I can't imagine anything easier than saying the words "I love you." However, for whatever reasons, many people simply don't do so. Perhaps we don't believe that our loved ones need to hear it, that they don't want to, or that they won't believe it. Or perhaps we're too stubborn or too shy. Whatever the reason, it's not good enough. There are simply too many important reasons to tell the people in your life that you love them.

Whether you heard these words enough in your own life or not is not the issue. At issue here is the fact that saying "I love you" makes people feel good. It reminds them that they are not alone and that you care. It raises their self-esteem—and it makes *you* feel good too! Undoubtedly, in my family, we do many things wrong. One thing we do right, however, is tell each other how much we love each other. It's simple, painless, and free. It's one of the most powerful sentences in the world. People who know they are loved (because they have been told) are able to offer the world their love in return. They have a quiet confidence and a sense of inner peace.

One of my firmest beliefs is that when you have what you want (in an emotional sense), your natural inclination is to give back to others. So, by saying "I love you" to a single person, you are, indirectly, helping the world at large. There is perhaps no way to guarantee that someone will feel loved and appreciated. But certainly the way to increase the odds is to tell him or her so, frequently. Genuinely saying the words "I love you" can erase many mistakes in the eyes of your loved ones. I know, for example, that when I've had difficult times with my kids, remembering to tell them I love them has helped us to forgive one another and move on.

On a more selfish note, saying "I love you" has personal benefits as well. It feels good. Since giving and receiving are two sides of the same coin, saying the words "I love you" more than makes up for not hearing them enough throughout your lifetime. It's absolutely true that giving is its own reward. And saying these loving words is one of the most basic and simple forms of giving.

There are so many opportune times to express your love in this manner—when you enter the house, right before you leave, before bed, and first thing in the morning. In our family, we have developed the habit of saying "I love you" before hanging up the telephone when we're talking to one another, as well as before we begin eating a family meal. Your opportunities are unlimited. This will be one of the easiest things you ever do—and, when all is said and done, one of the most important.

18.

Explore Voluntary Simplicity

There is a popular, grassroots movement that is quickly gaining momentum, finding its way to many diverse groups of people. This movement is called Voluntary Simplicity. As the name suggests, it involves simplifying one's life by choice rather than out of need. It means you put a ceiling on your desires, not necessarily because you have to but because you want to—you see the wisdom and potential for peace in placing a ceiling on what you want so that you can enjoy what you already have. Simplifying your life frees up time, money, and energy so that you can have more of each for yourself and for your family.

Interestingly enough, this movement toward a slightly simpler life is not limited to the super-wealthy. Instead, its wisdom is seen by a wide range of people from vastly different economic circumstances. I know a number of people with very limited incomes who have chosen to embrace this philosophy, and in every case, they claim it has paid handsome personal dividends.

Sometimes, simplifying your life can involve major shifts like choosing to live in a smaller, less expensive apartment rather than struggling to pay for a larger one. This decision can make your life less stressful because it will be far easier to pay your rent. Other common decisions involve things like eating more simply, sharing and passing on clothes to others, or saying no to more opportunities to do things. The idea, of course, is to make decisions that enhance your life in the possibly trips to the mechanic. Having fewer things means less things to take care of, insure, think about, worry about, and keep clean. Every item you purchase on credit is more to pay for, but is also one more bill to pay each month. Having a home with a yard involves gardening and time to care for it. I could go on, but I'm sure you get the picture. Voluntary Simplicity is not about giving up everything you own. To the contrary, there are obviously certain instances when obtaining (rather than getting rid of) something makes your life easier and simpler. For example, I can't imagine giving up my computer or fax machine. To do so would clearly make my life far more complicated and difficult. In fact, without my computer, I doubt very much that you'd be reading this book right now!

Voluntary Simplicity is not about any single decision, nor is it about voluntary poverty. You can drive an expensive car and still be committed to simplicity. You can enjoy, have, or even want nice things and still enjoy a simpler life. It's more of a direction, a series of conscious decisions that you make because you want to improve the quality of your life. The key is to take an honest look at what's truly important in your life. If you'd like a little more time, a little more energy, and a little more peace of mind, I encourage you to explore this topic a little more carefully.

19.

Don't Put Yourself Down

It's sad, but true: A good percentage of us engage in the negative habit of putting ourselves down and/or being overly self-critical. We'll say (or think) things like "I'm too fat," "I'm not good," or "I never do anything right." Do you ever engage in this unnecessary, yet all-too-common tendency?

The problem with putting yourself down is that, no matter how wonderful you actually are or how many positive qualities you have, you'll *always* find verification of that which you're looking for. In other words, there is a tendency, in all of us, to find that which we assume to be true regardless of what that assumption happens to be, that you'll find evidence that you are correct, making it equally predictable that you'll contribute to decreased self-esteem and negative feelings. Putting yourself down also reinforces, rather than corrects, your imperfections by putting unnecessary attention and energy on everything that's wrong, rather than what's right, with you. An important question to consider is, Why would you do this, knowing that the only *possible* result is a more negative outlook, more negative feelings, and less appreciation for the beautiful gift of life? Putting yourself down also makes you sound, to others, as if you feel like a victim of some kind. People who regularly put themselves down are often seen by others as complainers who lack appreciation for their lives, not to mention the example they set to their children, family, and friends. I hope I'm beginning to convince you that putting yourself down is a really bad idea with some rather severe personal consequences.

Obviously, everyone has aspects of themselves that they could, or would like to, improve upon. For example, one of the *many* things I would love to do is to become far more patient. At times, I feel I'm too reactive and easily bothered (in fact, I'm certain this is the case). But this *doesn't* mean that I should beat myself up and put myself down simply because I acknowledge that I'm far from perfect. Doing so would only reinforce this problem and make me feel worse than I already do about this issue. Knowing that I have plenty of room for improvement and making the decision and personal commitment to continue working toward my goal of increased patience is the best I can do. The more forgiving and patient I am with myself, the easier it will be for me to stay on my path of the money we do have. We dream about that special vacation we might or might not ever get to take, or that larger apartment we'd like to move into, but fail to do the smaller, yet equally enjoyable, things that we *can* afford to do, or make the best of the apartment we already have.

I have a good friend who has a very limited amount of money. It's amazing to me all that he has been able to do given his supply of available resources. He loves to take day trips and is inspired by camping. He has shown me some of the most beautiful photos of places I never knew existed. He has been on some of the most gorgeous hikes imaginable and the most incredible picnics ever. He enjoys rock climbing, flowers, birds, and sea life. He is one of the most inspiring and worldly people I've ever met, yet he rarely leaves the state. He has shown me that in our home state of California you can visit a beautiful, different place, within easy driving distance, every weekend—and never visit the same place twice if you don't want to. He chuckles at all the people he knows who have taken out bank loans to travel to exotic places like Europe but who have never seen a single state park right here near home. I've know my friend for over a decade and have never heard him complain *once* about a lack of money. In my mind, he's one of the "wealthiest" people on earth.

You can take this same mind-set and apply it to everything else where a lack of money *could* be seen as an obstacle. You can complain that you can't afford to move to a larger apartment or that you may never be able to buy your own home, or you can fix up your existing home in creative and inexpensive ways with the budget you already have. You can feel bad that you can't afford to buy your relatives the expensive Christmas gifts you'd like to get them, or you can feel proud of the meal or cookies you make for them or the beautiful card you took the time to pick out. It's up to each of us to decide for ourselves. Do we yearn for more and postpone our joy out of a lack of money—or do we make the best of it and keep our positive attitude intact?

Whenever we think more about what we don't have or can't do than about what we do have or can do, we create a gap between what we have and what we want. So often, this gap is the source of a great deal of stress. You can eliminate this source of stress by making the decision to stop using a lack of money to justify your unhappiness or boredom. This doesn't mean that you don't want or deserve more— or that you shouldn't try to get more. It merely suggests that, in the meantime, you enjoy as much as possible that which you already have. You may be surprised. If you put more attention on what you can do than what you can't do, one thing's for sure—you're going to have a lot more fun.

21

Make a List of Your Personal Priorities

I'll warn you in advance that this strategy can be humbling, but ultimately very helpful. It involves taking a careful look at those personal things that you feel are most important to you. Once you decide what they are, write them down on a sheet of paper and put the list away for a week or two.

For example, you might create a list that looks something like this: 1. pleasure reading, 2. exercise, 3. volunteering my time, 4. spending time with my family or close friends, 5. meditation, 6. spending time in nature, 7. getting organized, 8. writing in my journal, 9. trying something new, 10. eating healthy, 11. traveling.

Here's the hard part: after some time has gone by, take out your list and read it to yourself. Now, think back honestly over the past week or so, back to the time you wrote the list. How have you spent your time, other than the time you were working? If your actions over the past few weeks were consistent with your list, congratulations! You are in a tiny minority, and my only suggestion is to encourage you to keep it up. My guess is that you are fairly satisfied in your life, and that satisfaction spills over into your work life.

If, however, you look at your list and realize (as I did the first time I did this exercise) that a staggering percentage of your time was spent doing other things, then you've got work to do. If you're like most people, you probably got little or no exercise, didn't get around to volunteering, and spent all your time inside. To varying degrees, we ignore that which we insist is more important in favor of things that seem pressing or are simply more convenient. Unfortunately, life isn't going to suddenly accommodate us with fewer demands or reward us with the time we wish we had to do these important things. If we don't line up our behavior with our priorities, it will never happen.

A friend of mine taught me a powerful lesson that I always try to remember. He said, "In reality, you vote with your actions, not your words." This means that while I can tell you that my friends and family are important to me, I can write well-intended lists, and I can even become defensive in my well-thought-out excuses, ultimately, the measure of what's most important to me is how I spend my time and energy.

To put it bluntly, if I spend my free time washing my car, drinking in bars, and watching TV, then presumably my car, alcohol, and my TV are what's most important to me.

This isn't to say there is anything wrong with these activities—it's just important to admit to yourself that this is how you've been spending your time. It's also not to say that there aren't times when watching TV, even washing the car, is the most important thing to you at that moment. Again, that's fine. What I'm referring to here are your patterns of behavior, the way you spend most of your time.

You can see why this exercise is potentially so important to the quality of your life. When you're busy and working hard, tired and overwhelmed, it's easy to postpone or overlook your true priorities. You can get so lost in your routine and busyness that you end up doing few or none of the things that, deep down, you know would nourish you. You tell yourself things like, "This is a particularly busy time," or "I'll get to it later," but you never get around to it. This lack of satisfaction translates into frustration at work and elsewhere.

Once you open your eyes to the pattern, however, it's fairly easy to change. You can begin to make minor adjustments. You can read a few minutes before you go to sleep, get up a little earlier to exercise, meditate, or read. And so on. Remember, you're the one who wrote the list of priorities. You certainly have the power to implement them. I encourage you to write your list today—it really can create a whole new beginning.

22

Stop Procrastinating

Recently I received a frantic phone call from an accountant that demonstrates one of the most widely used excuses for being late. She used the familiar statement, "It was really complicated and took a great deal of time." If you take a deep breath and a step back, I think you'll agree with me that, in a way, this is a ridiculous excuse that creates unnecessary grief for both the person being late, as well as the person who has to wait. All it really does is ensure that you'll continue to be late, as well as encourage you to feel victimized by a shortage of time.

Every project takes a certain amount of time. This is true whether it's a tax form, other paperwork, a report, the building of a house, or the writing of a book. And, although factors that are well beyond our control and completely unpredictable do come into play, the truth is, in a vast majority of cases, you can make a *reasonable* estimate of the amount of time you will need to complete the task even if you have to factor in some extra time for unknown elements.

For example, the accountant I'm referring to was well aware that there was some measure of complexity to her task and that she would have to factor the degree of difficulty into her time schedule. She also had the advantage, as the rest of us do, of knowing the exact date that Uncle Sam demands the complete return! Why then did she wait so long to begin? And why did she use the "really complicated" excuse instead of simply admitting that she waited too long to get started? It would have taken her exactly the same number of hours to complete the project, whether she had started a month earlier or had she waited even longer.

Many of us do the very same thing in our work as well as in our personal lives. I know plenty of people who are virtually *always* late, whether it's to pick up the kids in their car pool, sit down before church starts on Sunday, or prepare food for dinner guests. The interesting part of this tendency isn't the fact that they are always running late, but the excuses that are used: "I had to pick up three kids," "I had to make two stops before work," "It's tough to get everything done before I run out the door,"

"Having dinner guests is more work for me."

Again, I'm not denying that it is tough to get everything done—it is—but in all of these examples, you are working with absolutely known variables. You know exactly how many kids you have, how long it takes to get them ready and to get them where they need to be. You know how long it takes to drive to work, and that there will almost certainly be traffic to contend with. You are absolutely aware of the fact that having dinner guests can be a lot of work, and that it takes a certain amount of extra time to prepare dinner and get everything ready. When we use the "I didn't have enough time" excuse we are fooling ourselves, thus virtually guaranteeing that we will make the identical mistake next time.

To get over this tendency requires humility.

wouldn't have been able to do my best job. Yet this is precisely what many people do in their work. They wait too long to begin, then complain about how much else they had going on.

Think of how much less stress would be in your life if you would simply begin your tasks a little earlier. Then rather than rushing from one project to the next, you'd have plenty of time. Rather than gripping the wheel and swerving your way from lane to lane to the airport or office, you'd arrive with a few minutes to spare. Rather than having the parents of the kids in your carpool angry and frustrated at you some, if not most of the time, you'd develop a reputation as a reliable and conscientious friend.

This is one of the simplest suggestions I've made in any of my books, yet in some ways it's one of the most important. Once you get in the habit of starting a little earlier, a great deal of your daily stress, at least that portion that you have some degree of control over, will fade away.

23

Forgive Yourself; You're Human

One of my favorite quotes is, "To err is human, to forgive divine." You might as well insert the word "yourself" into this all-so-true observation about being human. Let's face it. We are human, and to be human means you're going to make errors, at least some of the time. You're going to make plenty of mistakes, mess up from time to time, lose your way, forget things, lose your temper, say things you shouldn't have, and all the rest. I've never understood why this simple fact of life—our tendency to make mistakes—is so surprising or disappointing to people. I certainly don't understand why it's such a big deal.

To me, one of the saddest mistakes we make is a lack of forgiveness, especially to ourselves. We constantly remind ourselves of our flaws and previous mistakes. We anticipate future mistakes. We're highly critical of ourselves, frequently disappointed, and ruthless in our self-judgment. We badger and blame ourselves, and often we're our own worst enemy.

It seems to me that to be unforgiving of yourself is foolish and ridiculous. Life didn't come with a fool-proof manual. Most of us are doing the best that we can—really. But we're not perfect. The truth is, we're a work-in-progress. We learn from our mistakes and from stumbling. The best any of us can do, in any given moment, is to call it as we see it, to give it our best shot. None of us, however, certainly not I, have mastered life.

I'm sure that one of the reasons I'm a happy person is that I'm very forgiving of my mistakes. Someone recently asked me how I learned to be so kind to myself. My response was, "Because I've made so many mistakes, I've had lots of practice." She laughed, but it's actually true—I have had lots of practice! I can assure you, however, that my mistakes are not intentional. I truly do the best that I can. My work ethic as well as my standard of excellence is as high as most people's. So my forgiving attitude toward myself has nothing to do with any sort of apathy or a lowering of standards. It's more a matter of being realistic. Like almost everyone else, I have a great number of responsibilities. In fact, it usually seems like I'm juggling ten or twenty balls in the air simultaneously. So to assume I'll never make mistakes is absurd.

Can you sense how framing mistakes in this more realistic way gets you off the hook? In other words, when you make a mistake—even a stupid one—this more philosophic outlook allows you to keep your perspective and sense of humor instead of beating yourself. up. Instead of saying to yourself, "What an idiot," you'll be able to say, "More proof that I'm human."

Jack is a broker for a large financial institution. About a decade ago, a client specifically asked him to invest his life savings in a little stock called Intel! Jack, conservative by nature, convinced his client that it's never a good idea to invest in individual stocks, even at his client's relatively young age of 45. Jack felt it would be a better idea to put all the money in mutual funds.

Obviously, in this specific instance, Jack's

advice cost his client a fortune. Jack had given the same advice to a number of other people, and he became despondent and self-destructive. He lost his self-confidence and eventually changed careers. All this because he simply couldn't forgive himself. His friends, colleagues, even his clients, tried to convince him that his judgment and rationale at the time were solid—and that, by most standards, his clients had all done exceptionally well. He should be proud. When someone is unforgiving of himself, however, logic isn't usually received with an open mind.

Luckily, at some point, he hooked up with a good therapist who taught him the obvious— that everything is much clearer in hindsight and that no one has a crystal ball. Eventually, he was able to forgive himself and return to the career he had loved—financial planning.

Obviously, some mistakes are big. An air-traffic control mistake or one wrong move by a surgeon can be deadly. A vast majority of the mistakes we make, however, are not life or death; they are nothing more than "small stuff" disguised as "big stuff." It's true that even small mistakes can cause inconvenience, conflict, or extra work—and, as in the previous example, can be expensive—but what else is new? When did life suddenly become convenient or trouble-free?

While no one enjoys making mistakes, there is something very freeing about learning to accept them—really accept them—as an unavoidable part of life. When we do, we can forgive ourselves, thus erasing all the stress that usually results from badgering ourselves. So